Giving Myself over to J.S. Bach

Giving Myself Over to J.S. Bach

Poems by

Toni Ortner

Kelsay Books

Cover by Judith Kerman

ISBN: 978-1-947465-84-8

Kelsay Books
Aldrich Press
www.kelsaybooks.com

This book is a tribute to Elizabeth Bishop. The first lines of a few poems are taken from The Complete Poems of Elizabeth Bishop 1927-1979.

Acknowledgements

Some of the poems included in this book have appeared in their original forms in the journals listed below.

"I can make out the rigging of another schooner," Vol. 1 Redstart 4, 1987.

"For the first time I understand," Redstart 4 Plus, 1987.

"Performance is the thing you taught," Redstart 4 Plus, 1987.

"Protest," Maryland Poetry Review, winter, 1987.

"O to Burn a Perfect Arc in Space," Maryland Poetry Review, winter, 1987.

I dreamed that dead and meditating," Mudfish 2, Box Turtle Press, spring, 1987.

"This is the time of year," Mudfish 2, Box Turtle Press, spring, 1987.

"Dawn, an unsympathetic yellow," Redstart 4 Plus, 1987.

"Yes, the dead birds fell," Redstart 4 Plus, 1987.

"If you know where to set every stone," Black Sun, New Moon, Special Women's Issue, The Carolina Wren Press, 1980.

"Japanese Series," Vermont Literary Review, summer, 2010.

"Cutting the Blue Hydrangeas" "What You Said, Father"
Write Action 10th Anniversary Anthology, fall, 2010.

"Overnight the river removed its thick coat of ice"
"WHAT WILL THE PIGS DISCOVER WHEN THEY RAID
YOUR ISLAND?-Vermont Views Magazine, September, 2010.

"I don't want to dazzle you" plus Poem l and "Learn the rules"
Vermont Literary Review, summer, 2011.

Contents

I am in need of love that would flow naturally
like blood through veins
causing neither swelling, hemorrhage, nor pain.

I am in need of love like water
pours silken over rocks.

The dream is
as if love had no stops to block
all smooth fingering
as if love were all melody and harmony
as if love could continue
its contiguous smooth undulation towards the sea
though we know how unruly, unpredictable,
wild a river it can be
as if there could be no vessels capsized   no contours altered
no masts splintered   nothing sucked under.

Protest

March
the trees stand stiff as pubescent girls stripped of camouflage
that green necessity of petticoats and lace.

Sunlight caresses the bark slowly   merciless as a tongue
lacquers each ice-coated branch with promises.
The wind blows in gusts from the North at regular intervals.

The sunlight makes the roots tremble
branches doubt sanity and sequence.

Who were you to enter my life unbidden
each smile a caress   your eyes promising a change of season
light beyond expectation or reason
vanishing silent   swift   blameless as a cloud
while I remain rooted
remembering a smile as merciless as the sunlight.

March memory blue ash & shadowed long against
the blood stained crust of snow
coating leafless trees like a woman's wedding gown
draped in soundless folds about the trunks torn to tatters.

They said in the Russian tale the bride was hurled off the sled
by the groom
so that it might go faster
hurled into the mouths of hungry howling wolves.

He hopes to escape with a wild easy rush of air into another village
where no one would recognize him as Faithful Groom.
He believed it that easy to shift identity.
Instead the sled's weight   unbalanced   shifted   tipped over.

Emboldened by your lies, others' smiles
you race forwards towards imagined freedom
yet the both of us have long since died.

You died the instant the thought crossed your mind
"Throw her to the wolves so I can survive."

The villagers heard the howling.
In the morning they discovered two skeletons   not even bones
touching.

End

Now you see the monument/now you don't.
It is stitched in silence letter by letter
under an immutable lead sky.
It says Sudan. It says Darfur. It says Leningrad.

Now you see the monument/now you don't.

.

A ray of sunlight
lights the blood stained crust of snow
as if they had survived.

Now you see the monument/now you don't.

It is made of grief
woven from the tangled filaments of
half remembered dreams that haunt the days
like ghosts.

Now you see the monument/now you don't.

Land lies in water shadowed green.
Does the sea in its liquidity recede from the hard-contoured
embrace of land
then eager to kiss swing back in heavy tides
to brush its velvet hips
like a somnambulist.

Such approaches & retreats.
Such hesitancy & doubts.
Such a minute of ripples& sunlight.
When our eyes met for an instant
it's definitive.

Daytona Beach Dawn 1949

Smooth white sand licks the sea
inseparable as you believe families to be.

Mother father son daughter
walk slowly amid the shells and stones,
rays of sunlight turned to golden jewels.

Everything breathes respite
suspended out of time or reason
as in a many chambered Nautilus shell.

A red buoy rings its bell.
Thick fog floats in, whispering hush don't you cry,
tiny sandpipers caught between sea and sky.

No shipwrecks here
just a gentle lullaby.

The black Packard with the rumble seat is safely parked in a lot.

STOP

You have a long journey ahead.
Remember Daytona Beach.

I can make out the rigging of another schooner
sailing past my desk out the door into fields
over brown hills stripped of any semblance of grass.

It is clear they are headed east
towards the sea
a long slow procession
sailors in yellow slickers
valiantly trying to raise sail.

But there is no wind here on stark brown hills
filled with mud puddles   abandoned cars
pieces of sodden cardboard.
Rain slashes down like knives across the heart
parting doorframes
splintering windows
where I watch the long slow procession of schooners
sailing across stark brown hills
filled with mud puddles.

Daddy promised we would sail around the world.
He would be Skipper and I would be Cook.
Every night he turned the pages of Yachting like a Bible
on his lap
searching for schooners for sale.
"Don't tell the child such tales," mother called inside
wiping red eyes in the kitchen
after a rendezvous with her lover.

"You are my best girl," Daddy whispered in my ear.
Something I definitely did not wish to hear.

Moon

The moon in the mirror
is not made of cheese like children believe.

The moon in the mirror has no face
except the one you superimpose.

The moon in the mirror is not a stage set
as if life is a film and you the blond heroine.

The moon in the mirror belongs to no one.
All the wishes you made
dissipated in space like shreds of lace.
It never cared for songs like
"Blue moon I saw you standing alone"
& all that rot and the way songs
picture it watching people
fall in and out of love
as if its function is to be a mirror.

The moon waxes and wanes moves tides of sea salt blood
indifferent to the men who walk its surface stick flags in.

The moon in the mirror is a reflection
trapped inside its skin
beyond projection or metaphor
resembles you.

In the dark of the moon
a musician is driving.
On the back seat his reeds
chaste and lovely locked in cases
wait for his lips so they may speak.

He dreams of a season where it is always summer
windows open
tires humming a comfortable small tune
a case of ice cold beer within reach.
      What crime can he have committed
      to endure incessant grief
      forced to swallow it in bitter teaspoonfuls.

He thinks of his unfaithful wife
a life he might have led
a song he would write if notes
could find a clear space.

Who is to say which highway is real
the one he dreams
or the one he rides?

Rosa Ibarra still missing smiles hopefully
from a faded poster on the wall
in a hallway in a building ten thousand miles away
from her own country

where the daily butchering of human beings
chopped off heads and testicles is taken for granted
features seared off faces   God in absentia.

There one dares not venture out after dark
or fish familiar rivers lest one cast one's innocent hook into flesh.

Too many bodies and no one to stand accused.

Rosa Ibarra a peasant
who never knew she would become so famous
smiles hopefully from a faded poster on the wall
ten thousand miles from her own country
where unidentified bodies are the broken pieces of our dreams
cast into ditches.

I dreamed that dead and meditating I met you in a different life.
We had lost our given names. You had relinquished your wife.
Gender made no difference. I was no longer the writer.
You were no longer the musician.

      Finally it was clear and unequivocal
      we were the same species
      equal halves rejoined to form a perfect whole.

It was on a vast plain under a star that never set
in a world without shadows to define light
where we could breathe an atmosphere pure and bright
devoid of grief.
Naked in spirit and relief
our bodies became what we formerly believed was music
each note sufficient onto itself contained the entire range of notes
alto   bass   soprano.
Scales flowed slowly into one another like water
unbroken in intent
eddying of its own accord past all given obstacles
 to return to its source.

We melted into one another instantaneous with thought
love sparked   startling   spangled   profane past prayer.

O to burn a perfect arc in space
as naturally as sun and mirror left to their own devices
ignite in flame   sear wood to ash.

To move towards one another
magnetized like iron filings
against their separate intellects or wills
by a law they bend obedient to but never comprehend.

To enclose the past by the present
as if it were a walled garden and we had stepped outside
for a breath of fresh air and locked the gate behind.

To My Father, before his triple bypass surgery

Dawn, yellow paler than skin sickened by a bout of malaria
rises thin and gaunt against the white sky
light so fevered it dazzles and blinds the eyes.

A breeze rushes in straight from the sea
like a madman shouting a message to save the world.

You stand on the balcony looking down.
I stand directly beneath on a patch of sodden ground
so you can see without shifting.

. You gaze at me as if this is an ordinary day.
It is no longer clear which one of us must go away.

What is unbearable to know
as the cab edges slowly away
is that under a sky as blue as this
your heart is more fragile than a robin's egg.

Biscayne Bay shines like a promise in the distance.

Can we hedge another bet old gambler?

Performance is the thing you taught.

The buildings rush by as the sun rises higher in the sky.

I arrive at the airport
step up the ramp
into the gaping jaw of the plane,
on automatic pilot head north.

For the first time I understand
what it means to drown in music.

I remember you sleeping thorough the days
with earphones on
an automaton.
We never questioned what you listened to.

Now I listen too
choose a voice to superimpose upon my own
Vivaldi's Four Seasons utterly melodic and composed
in its transitions from spring to winter.

Learning to let go
as if it was natural as breath.

Giving myself over to J.S. Bach
the ultimate seduction by a mind possessing amplitude of order
notes arranged assiduously balanced to form a perfect whole
like the intricately constructed boxes of Joseph Cornell
in which he made do using anything at hand
boxes within boxes
everything inside one could need or imagine an approximation to.

The chaos I lived through losing you lies like silt
 at the edge of the moving tide.

I sense it may lead me to an immense still body
in whose breast I will reside.

Violating Your Boundaries

Wasted minutes
staring at the leafless branch of a tree
incipient snow hovering in the January air.

"What did I say," he asked
a victim of sudden amnesia
shifting direction by specifics.

Her answer would have made no difference.

Love to him was the Federal Crime
she stood convicted of a priori
the emotion he refused
to acknowledge
under any circumstances, however extenuating
lest he be tumbled into happiness
something he
would never encompass or permit.

She has learned her lesson well
can thrive on one smile
decorate hell.

The fox said he did not want the grapes.

What a senseless waste to face a wall.

Self preservation should have taught the fox the taste of mangoes
so he could dance the gay fandango.

For Elizabeth Bishop

Elizabeth, I cast your lines
out into each day
watch your syllables float, still on the surface,
to mark the spot until the sinker drops.

The line grows taut in an instant
tugged hard from beneath
pulled deep by a force I cannot see but sense.

I open up the bail
& in a shot you're off
line skimming fast through my fingers
tugging the whole damn boat of rhyme behind
as if it was a joke.

Rushing towards an unknown destination
scarf blowing in the wind
I steer a course past grief
until a song
begins to sing its own vibration
singular   clear   unbroken.

We pass the last island
whose boundaries I thought I knew
now all blue speeding through the open channel
I have become for you.

The state with the prettiest name
was the minute I stepped through your door
& you turned with a face tender   waiting   open.
That hesitation the minuet of love
unspoken,
the dance unbroken
before the grief of speech
stopped us in motion.

Bell Hollow Road

The mended fence is gone. Wood is turned to rot.
No one remembers the house that stood on this spot.
Stones from the wall lie, seized by the elements.
The inhabitants' blue ash sifts finely through the thin April air.

This is the time of year as one grows older one begins to fear.
Everything that hibernated in the cold
begins to let go   liquefy   seduced by promise.

The unequivocal sum of years approaches like a solstice
 like destiny.
The sky formerly content to be white and distant as God
softens too   not of its own volition
becomes an acquiescent blue   daydreams of tornadoes
receptive to anything   most certainly a dangerous mood
especially for the intellect.

Air grows ears
it did not formerly possess
to catch the budding insects' hum.

Strangers burst into song for no apparent reason.
It's the season limbs loosen as if gravity were not the law we live
by.
Confusion becomes not only acceptable but delicious.
Everything alive cannot help but start to sing and stretch.
There is greed a violent incipient need to strip off layer after layer
as if it were a dare.

April is the cruelest month. A month of promises.
I remember you playing "April in Paris where shall I run to"
that closed door I flung myself against for months
until my flesh turned black and blue. Anorexic for love.

You
your silent mouth
the only star in heaven I could have sworn by
followed over every goddamned continent and sea like the fabled
Magi.

When a conundrum of Love propounded you to me,
I proposed to gladly abdicate my identity
as if you were the source of gravity
drawing me irresistibly as a magnet sweeps up iron filings
or lemmings rush headlong towards the sea.

When a conundrum of Love propounded you to me
unmeasured desire unhinged the intellect;
sexuality became a pack of starved wolves.

Sex cannot appease a buried need
grown insatiable as greed.

In such a season of starvation
a conundrum of Love propounded you to me.

When I remember you
I think about Egyptian mummies
how the flesh crumbles to dust
when exposed to touch
how artifacts are not the real thing
how illusion works by distance
how the heart released can sing.

The air is bright and dazzles
when one has eyes to see
past grief.

Effort distills and sugars despair;
makes it palatable for the intellect to swallow and bear.
Music has become the sacred ground
through soundless dreams
missed trains   cars without drivers careening wildly
a stranger's bloodless suicide.
I thought our chords were synchronized;
the timing was off.

You remain an ineffable enigma
an ancient skull that sings and talks
astonishing sex the stigmata of the flesh
that will not wash off.

I keep company with my mirror
pull a comb listless through my hair.

Imagination will not make the ultimate leap
summon up your image
intact as Icarus before the fall.

When the liquid light of summer retreats
left with the measure of all intended
love falls short.

What was it that stopped you all those years
you yanked the reins too short
dug your heels into flanks
to make horse and rider rear.

If the line found its own speed,
it might drag you behind.

When you let the horse run
it finds its own pace and stride
not for show, ribbons won, pride.

It is a wild untrammeled gallop through open fields over fences
until rider and horse covered with sweat spin slowly to a halt.

No master exists who can prepare the rider for the final run.

As far as statues go there is not a single one I know
that moves and breathes
regardless of the artist's need.

To graft a dream to flesh is at best
a tenuous procedure filled with risk.

When love fades
the intellect steps in with grave precision
sharp as a scalpel cuts emotion's loss
snips off badly sewn stitches,
so nothing is left but bruises.

The artist returns alone to face clay and stone.

But O the light lost.

On the failure of language to conjugate

Transcribing one language for another
to decipher the other's intentions.

Translations miss the mark.

What was it he said and what was it she meant?
Can when be removed from if?

The nouns refuse to metamorphose into verbs.
What is said is never what is heard.
The verbs will not take on the adulations
of whimpering adjectives.

The sum is more than the parts.

Yes, the dead birds fell but no one had seen them fly.
They must have flown; otherwise, they could not
drop sudden from the sky
like heavy stones or hail out of season
forcing the viewer to doubt his reason.

One cannot ascertain whether the melodies
were composed of ecstasy or pain;
indeed, the incident remains strange.

One wants to believe it never occurred.
One hopes the evidence will vanish
so there is nothing left to question.

How long the notes were held
how sweet the infinite gradations in modulation.

There are whole acts we miss as the final curtain descends.

The dead birds fell but no one had seen them fly.

During the Time I Tried to Forget the Color of Grief

Around the edge of the path
at intervals of nine feet
wooden benches to sit and rest
watch others walk around
watching their feet.

Inside those thick walls
you could not hear the noises of the street.

Everyone wore gray uniforms with white stripes
provided by the state.
Careful not to step on ants,
I walked away each day
between the hours of two and three
wanting to leap
into the East River beneath.

The old man
lifted up the gowns of young ladies
told us how when he was a young man
he did if fifty times a night even screwed a sheep.

Transformation occurs
when the mind records experience
the way it prefers
to remember
conveniently
omits
intimate details
known
by the senses.

Dear Mother,

I admit I was never the laughing blond cherub you wanted.

These are my flowers
a bouquet of black and white letters.

May I sit you down at a stanza?
It is not pink.

This poem for Mother's Day
contains no hearts, flowers, lace
thirty-nine years locked together,
opposite sides of the same face.

Anchored to this massive desk
I write poems on your neatly sewn stitches
embroider your dreams.

Mother, this morning I am tired.
I want to come home
touch my lips
to the seam in your chest
that held your breasts.

Thunder rumbles over the mountain
the heat a black veil in the still air.

Thunder rumbles over the mountain
where rhododendron leaves droop like limp hands.

A crow caws.　A cat slinks by with a blank stare.
Yellow and black butterflies
conference with beating wings.

Last August like this
only wounds.

Thunder rumbles over the mountain.
I lie still, deeply dreaming.

A scarlet bird streaks towards the sun.

Love Poem for Stephen

Tulips leaves unfurl thin green flags.

Yellow daffodils bloom as they did in our childhood.
Now our gratitude for each sun among the ferns.

Orange daylilies multiply.

White narcissus flares sweetly
 towards the sky's unmeasured space.
The sun strains through icy branches
burns our lined faces.

The dance of life continues in spite of our beliefs.
The hospital doors slam shut on the cold corpses.

Love remains the anchor.

Japanese Series

Striations of rock
waves in a stormy sea.

When I am dead
will an instant of my mind
be etched between these lines?

In any ceremony it is important not to rush.
Anticipation
makes the cherry blossoms brighter
the green tea more pungent on the tongue.

A branch softly bent
assumes its most beautiful shape.

Space is never negative.

Wherever you are
you see the landscape in your head.

The scholar walking over the bamboo bridge
does not perceive
the cobra hanging from the tree.

Poem 1

White sand becomes a sea   you set sail
under a glaring sun
stones   islands dropped from the sky.

Precipitous cliffs rise up stark
from the ocean bed.

You sail on and on.
Waves of blue pebbles
ripple.

From the Japanese Stone Garden

Learn the rules.
Forget them.

Immerse yourself in one stone.
Let color, form, texture
direct you where to place it.

The finest poems
teach the poet.

I don't want to dazzle you
with words.
There comes a point in every art
when excellence is not enough.

What comes after
discovered.

If you
endeavor
to describe
the point on which you stand
steppingstones that led you there

           paper turned to ash.

Van Gogh in the Office

You place Van Gogh's irises on the wall.
The color of the petals too extravagant
stretch towards the edge of despair
press against the frame
veer wildly off the canvas as if there were no air.

So much remains unclear
after all these years,
true colors of petals or pain
what stains   what washes out what remains.

For Sunshine (killed May 29, 1983)

The sun which is not an eye and lacks commitment
manages to rise consistent.

I do what I must
sit on the back steps at dusk
gazing at your grave hidden by goldenrod
that spread violently all summer
as if a mad painter
smeared ochre all over a green palette.

That such a common weed flourishes is an affront.

The mauve sunset is artificial as imported roses in winter.

The tail you waved so bravely
returns in dreams
a white flag flashing me down into darkness
where we lay nestled arm over paw.

I picture you waiting, patient by our door.

September 15, 1983- March 17, 1987

In my dream we walk arm in arm through your orchard

rows of plum trees
you never expected to inherit
anymore than the Flower Garden quilt
stitched in Kansas.

You point out the twisted aged limbs
explain how none still birth fat purple plums
whose skin burst icy sweetness on your tongue.

"I had a beautiful childhood," you say.
Our mother's flesh reduced to ash
cast into air like votive offerings.

It is white and cold.
We float through the gnarled barren landscape pitted with craters
moving towards the dark we must explore.

A gray rabbit by the side of the road
head resting on an outstretched paw
in the still September air
white ears listening intently
to the buzz of bees
a chain saw.

The second leg white as a popsicle stick, crushed.

A gentle breeze stirs the dear soft hair.

The clear eyes fill slowly with bright light
spilled from beyond the mountains
of blue familiar.

White moths wings thinner than paper
press against the glass.
Let them fly into the cool autumn night.

We remain
pinned to illusion
longing for light
past time, season, rhyme, reason.

Let the page become my lover
receptive to each letter.

It never talks back or questions.
It accepts whatever I offer.

Hour after hour
I reveal more than I could give up bathed in sweat.

I am not writing for you.
I do not write for men.

The woman I write for is long since dead,
her black hair glistening silk.

She lies on my pillow each night
whispering words in my ears.

It is she who speaks through my fingers on these keys.
It is she to whom I offer these black bouquets.

You were mistaken if you believed I was your lover.

White petals
over the pond
the water keeps flowing
you are no longer
here.

December 27, 1988

For Lisa,

You like the winter's cold light clarifying edges
revealing shapes that lay hidden in greener seasons.

You want to turn now   face it all
stark whiteness stinging
sun glinting off a bare branch which shines like pale fire.

The red cardinal sits on the same branch singing

as if family could be retrieved
easy as a fish scooped into a net
from a hole cut in the ice

as if safety lay in sight.

What You Said, Father

The spring afternoon on the manicured lawn
after we had turned our deck chairs
to catch the last rays of sun
the orange azaleas and yellow daylilies
a freshly watered bouquet

you walked twenty feet
after being told by the surgeon you could not walk more than ten.
It was the second week after surgery
a tumor the size of a grapefruit in the left lobe of your lung.

The sky was never a cleaner brighter blue
as we sat in silence side by side.

I hold your freckled hand so large in mine.

I hold your freckled hand so large in mind.

March 7- March 21, 1993

Report to Daddy

You did not get the Benny Goodman or the dry martinis.
The Riverside Chapel in Hewlett was packed.

I shook hands with strangers
kept one eye on your coffin
where mother placed seven red roses.

Left alone I kneeled down
kissed your coffin like the Blarney Stone.

I wept all night in my lover's arms
while the wind wailed in Goose Bay.

January 21-22, 1993

Reynard the red fox
swift   elusive   cunning.

If women could breathe the souls of animals
I'd slip inside your bones and skin

skim across fields of snow
in the dark woods at night
where the moon shines bright on the ice.

A sharp cry wakens the dreamers.

Cutting the Blue Hydrangeas

My mother and I stand side by side.
She examines the sharpness of the shears
bows gently of grave necessity as in an ancient Chinese ceremony.

In that instant we metamorphose into sisters.

How many years have we stood together
to cut the blue hydrangeas?
How many gardens and houses float between us
in the warm September air?

"Always pick the most perfect blossoms.
  Discard any with brown edges.
  You must force the strength back into the roots.
  These when dried should last the entire winter.
  Put them in vases in all the rooms of your house.
  When you look at them, think of me."

A sudden gust of wind from Goose Bay
tears a leaf off an oak
intimating an icy winter.

Light has placed
a benediction upon us.

Peter Speaks

Seven days since you left;
I know you would have wanted me to eat.

There is Brie and Camembert, chocolate waffle wafers,
artichoke brochettes, poppy water crackers
to wash down with Bishop's Peak.

I cannot sleep.
I dream I meet you in a green field.
It is spring.
You are astonished by the heavy basket
of shiny red apples, perfect green grapes,
dates, nuts, figs, kiwis, star fruits, and strawberries.
"Is this for me?" you ask with a bemused smile.

The fruit is cut and shaped like a bouquet of flowers.

You would have wanted me to eat.
I open Tuscan garlic bread sticks, fudge truffles,
hazelnut biscotti, dipping pretzels,
baked parmesan, garlic and herb pita chips.

The Godiva chocolates
taste like ashes.

Remembering Toby

I am grateful for the clouds and rain.
Sun seems heresy.

I take Toto for a walk down by the bay.
Morning unravels like a dream.

Blowfish lumber slow examining crevices.
One with green eyes stares.
Needle fish cluster in pairs.

I kneel down by the shore in grief
watch a yellow leaf drift
through the autumn air.

A large tilapia coasts by indifferent
to my presence.

WHAT WILL THE PIGS DISCOVER WHEN THEY RAID
YOUR ISLAND?
(written beneath a bridge near the Brattleboro Co-op)

A house with eleven wind chimes
pink phlox growing in abandoned railroad tracks
no billboards

hemp clothes
thousands of books

hand made vases
fields of buttercups

the word peace
painted on rocks

an intersection of five lanes
with no stop light
where no one was killed

a sign offering free meals to the homeless
& shelter in winter

the Connecticut River
flowing quietly between high cliffs.

March 17, 2009 Brattleboro, Vermont

Overnight the river removed its thick coat of white.
Metallic blue shivers.

The current carries chunks of ice.
The bridge keeps its balance
against swift gusts.

Nine flocks of geese v northward.
The sun hovers low at the edge of the West
as if it never wants to set.

I know where I am
by four church steeples.

At dusk five sparrows perch on the thin bare branches of a bush,
sudden hush   lamplights lit.

A girl with long red hair carries a violin,
runs laughing up a steep flight of steps.

Two boys toss a baseball in a courtyard.

This is the world.
Faith demands
we cannot imagine it different.

About the Author

Toni Ortner lives in Putney, Vermont. In 2018 Fractured Woman and End Rhymes for End Times is being published by Word Tech Communications and Daybook I is scheduled for publication by Deerbrook Editions. On the fourth Sunday of each month she hosts the Write Action Radio Hour where she interviews writers and they read their work. Recent writing and reviews of her books are located at vermontviews.org under Old Lady Blog. She gives readings in bookstores and libraries.

www.ingramcontent.com/pod-product-compliance
Lightning Source LLC
LaVergne TN
LVHW021623080426
835510LV00019B/2740